G000242281

National Trus
Arts and Crafts
postcard book

First published in the United Kingdom in 2014 by
National Trust Books
10 Southcombe Street
London W14 0RA
An imprint of Anova Books Ltd

ISBN: 9781907892752

A CIP catalogue record for this book is available
from the British Library.

24 23 22 21 20 19 18 17 16 15 14
10 9 8 7 6 5 4 3 2 1

Reproduction by Rival Colour Ltd, UK
Printed by Main Choice Printing Ltd, China

This book can be ordered direct from the publisher at the
website: www.anovabooks.com, or try your local bookshop.
Also available at National Trust shops, including
www.nationaltrustbooks.co.uk. To buy prints of any of these
postcards, please visit www.ntprints.com.

National Trust
Arts and Crafts
postcard book

First published in the United Kingdom in 2014 by
National Trust Books
10 Southcombe Street
London W14 0RA
An imprint of Anova Books Ltd

ISBN: 9781907892752

A CIP catalogue record for this book is available
from the British Library.

24 23 22 21 20 19 18 17 16 15 14
10 9 8 7 6 5 4 3 2 1

Reproduction by Rival Colour Ltd, UK
Printed by Main Choice Printing Ltd, China

This book can be ordered direct from the publisher at the
website: www.anovabooks.com, or try your local bookshop.
Also available at National Trust shops, including
www.nationaltrustbooks.co.uk. To buy prints of any of these
postcards, please visit www.ntprints.com.

National Trust

Standen, East Grinstead
'Trellis' wallpaper (1862) by William Morris and
incorporating birds drawn by Philip Webb at Standen,
East Grinstead
National Trust Images/Jonathan Gibson

For more information visit
www.nationaltrust.org.uk
To buy a print visit **www.ntprints.com**
Registered Charity no. 205846 © National Trust

National Trust

Standen, East Grinstead
William de Morgan tile in the Billiard Room
at Standen, East Grinstead
National Trust Images/Jonathan Gibson

National Trust

Wightwick Manor, Wolverhampton
'Pomona' Tapestry watercolour design (1884) by
Edward Burne-Jones, background by William Morris
at Wightwick Manor, Wolverhampton
National Trust Images/Derrick E. Witty

National Trust

Wightwick Manor, Wolverhampton
William De Morgan lustreware plate
at Wightwick Manor, Wolverhampton

National Trust Images/Andreas von Einsiedel

National Trust

Wightwick Manor, Wolverhampton
'Leicester' wallpaper (c.1911) by J H Dearle for Morris
& Co. at Wightwick Manor, Wolverhampton

National Trust Images/Andreas von Einsiedel

National
Trust

Cragside, Rothbury
'Autumn' (1873), one of four stained-glass panels by
William Morris in the Dining Room at Cragside, Rothbury
National Trust Images/Andreas von Einsiedel

For more information visit
www.nationaltrust.org.uk
To buy a print visit **www.ntprints.com**
Registered Charity no. 205846 © National Trust

National
Trust

Wightwick Manor, Wolverhampton
'Acanthus' wallpaper (c.1875) by William Morris
at Wightwick Manor, Wolverhampton

National Trust Images/Andreas von Einsiedel

For more information visit
www.nationaltrust.org.uk
To buy a print visit **www.ntprints.com**
Registered Charity no. 205846 © National Trust

National
Trust

Wightwick Manor, Wolverhampton
'Pomegranate' wallpaper (1866) by William Morris
at Wightwick Manor, Wolverhampton

National Trust Images/Andreas von Einsiedel

National Trust

Wightwick Manor, Wolverhampton
'Pimpernel' Wallpaper (c.1876) by Morris & Co.
at Wightwick Manor, Wolverhampton

National Trust Images/Andreas von Einsiedel

For more information visit
www.nationaltrust.org.uk
To buy a print visit **www.ntprints.com**
Registered Charity no. 205846 © National Trust

National
Trust

Standen, West Sussex
'Bird' tapestry by William Morris at Standen,
West Sussex

National Trust Images/Jonathan Gibson

National Trust

Red House, Bexleyheath
William Morris tile inscribed 'Si je puis' ('If I can')
Morris' motto, at Red House, Bexleyheath
National Trust Images/Nadia Mackenzie

National
Trust

Wightwick Manor, Wolverhampton
William Morris 'Dove and Rose' silk and wool wall
hangings (c.1893) at Wightwick Manor, Wolverhampton
National Trust Images/John Hammond

National
Trust

Wightwick Manor, Wolverhampton
'Tulip and Trellis' ceramic tiles at Wightwick Manor,
Wolverhampton

National Trust Images/John Hammond

National
Trust

Wightwick Manor, Wolverhampton
William Morris 'Cray' pattern (c.1860s) curtains
at Wightwick Manor, Wolverhampton

National Trust Images/John Hammond

National
Trust

Wallington, Morpeth
William Morris wallpaper hung in 1897
for Lady Trevelyan at Wallington, Morpeth

National Trust Images/Andreas von Einsiedel

For more information visit
www.nationaltrust.org.uk
To buy a print visit **www.ntprints.com**
Registered Charity no. 205846 © National Trust

National Trust

Wightwick Manor, Wolverhampton
William de Morgan tiles at Wightwick Manor,
Wolverhampton

National Trust Images/Paul Raeside

National
Trust

Gunby Hall, Spilsby
'Daisy' wallpaper (c.1862) by William Morris,
at Gunby Hall, Spilsby
National Trust Images/Nadia Mackenzie

National Trust

Red House, Bexleyheath
Edward Burne-Jones' stained-glass window 'Fate'
at Red House, Bexleyheath

National Trust Images/John Hammond

National Trust

National
Trust

Wightwick Manor, Wolverhampton
'Fair Rosamund' by Henry Treffry Dunn
at Wightwick Manor, Wolverhampton

National Trust Images

National
Trust

Wightwick Manor, Wolverhampton
'The Rescue' by J R Spencer Stanhope
at Wightwick Manor, Wolverhampton

National Trust

National Trust

Wightwick Manor, Wolverhampton
'Love among the Ruins' (c.1894) by Edward Burne-Jones
at Wightwick Manor, Wolverhampton

National Trust

National Trust

National Trust

Wightwick Manor, Wolverhampton
'The Haunted Wood' by Elizabeth Eleanor Siddal
at Wightwick Manor, Wolverhampton

National Trust Images/Paul Highnam

For more information visit
www.nationaltrust.org.uk
To buy a print visit **www.ntprints.com**
Registered Charity no. 205846 © National Trust